Keats Lives

Moya Cannon was born in County Donegal, spent most of her adult life in Galway and now lives in Dublin. She is the author of four previous collections of poems, *Oar* (1990), *The Parchment Boat* (1997), *Carrying the Songs* (2007) and *Hands* (2011). She studied at University College, Dublin, and Corpus Christi College, Cambridge. A winner of the inaugural Brendan Behan Award and the Lawrence O Shaughnessy Award, she has edited *Poetry Ireland Review* and was 2011 Heimbold Professor of Irish Studies at Villanova University.

Also by Moya Cannon from Carcanet Press

Hands (2011)
Carrying the Songs (2007)

MOYA CANNON

Keats Lives

CARCANET

First published in Great Britain in 2015 by
Carcanet Press Limited
Alliance House, 30 Cross Street
Manchester, M2 7AQ

www.carcanet.co.uk

We welcome your comments:
info@carcanet.co.uk

A CIP catalogue record for this book is available from the British Library.

ISBN 978 1 784100 60 5

The publisher acknowledges financial assistance from Arts Council England.

Supported using public funding by
ARTS COUNCIL
ENGLAND

Contents

for Jim and Kathy Murphy

Winter View from Binn Bhriocáin

In the mountain-top stillness
the bog is heather-crusted iron.
A high, hidden mountain pond
is frozen into zinc riffles.

We have tramped across a plateau
of frost-smashed quartzite
to the summit cairn.

Far below, in February light,
lakes, bogs, sea-inlets,
the myriad lives being lived in them,
lives of humans and of trout,
of stonechats and sea-sedges
fan out, a palette of hammered silver,
grey and silver.

Two ivory swans

fly across a display case
as they flew across Siberian tundra
twenty thousand years ago,
heralding thaw on an inland sea –
their wings, their necks, stretched,
vulnerable, magnificent.

Their whooping set off a harmonic
in someone who looked up,
registered the image
of the journeying birds
and, with a hunter-gatherer's hand,
carved tiny white likenesses
from the tip of the tusk
of the great land-mammal,
wore them for a while,
traded or gifted them
before they were dropped
down time's echoing chute,
to emerge, strong-winged,
whooping,
to fly across our time.

(British Museum, April 2013)

Finger-fluting in Moon-Milk

We are told that usually, not always,
a woman's index-finger
is longer than her ring-finger,
that, in men, it is usually the opposite,
that the moon-milk in this cave
retains the finger prints and flutings
of over forty children, women and men
who lived in the late Palaeolithic.
Here, in the river-polished Dordogne,
as the last ice-sheets started to retreat
northwards from the Pyrenees,
in a cave which is painted
with long files of mammoths
and gentle-faced horses,
a woman, it seems, with a baby on her hip
trailed her fingers down through
the soft, white substance
extruded by limestone cave-walls
and the child copied her.
Today, the finger-flutings remain clear,
the moon-milk remains soft;
as we trundle through the cave's maze
in our open-topped toy train
we are forbidden to touch it.

With no gauge to measure sensibility
we cannot know what portion
of our humanity we share
with someone who showed a child
how to sign itself in moon-milk
one day, late in the Old Stone Age.

(Rouffignac, 2010)

11

Four thimbles

were sieved out of the mud of the riverbank
in the cloister of the convent of Santa Clara a Velha,
were dug out of silt with the convent itself
which had started to sink into Mondego waters
one year after the last stone carver had wiped the dust
off the twined leaves, off the doves
above the door capitals.

In May light, broad sandstone vaults
are sand-blasted, clean as stones fallen
from glacial till at the sea's edge –
clean of mud, of candle smoke,
almost of history.

For seven hundred years the waters rose,
drowning the blue-tiled fountain and the cloister gardens.
The nuns raised and raised the church floor
until psalms were sung high among the vaults.
Finally, they built on higher ground.
Farm horses were stabled in the nave,
the rose window became a farmhouse door.

Four battered silver thimbles
were dredged up with needles, scissors,
broken crockery,
cloister tiles.

Crossed lovers,
widowed noblewomen
or peasant girls who placed them
on middle or ring fingers,
who bent their heads
to stitch plain habits or fine altar linen
were sisters, but only

as stars are sisters,
who form a constellation
but inhabit different planes and eons.
Their stitching talk was
of treachery and love betrayed,
clanking crusades, inquisitions, dynasties
on the rise or on the wane,
new worlds to the west
full of gold and murder,
of fresh bread, olives and always
the rising waters.

Small things survive inundations –
thimbles,
blue tiles,
doves.

(Coimbra, 2013)

'Beware of the Dog'

Cave Canem,
the threshold mosaic warned
but not *Cave Montem;*
although there had been earthquakes,
no one suspected the mountain,
or understood the shunt and dive
of the earth's plates.
or the burning tides that drive them.

With a long wooden spatula
Celer, the baker, the slave
of Quintus Granius Verus,
slid this round wholemeal loaf,
with both of their names
branded into it,
from the brick oven
hours or minutes before
ash fell like hot snow
and hid their city.

(British Museum, 2013)

Burial, Ardèche 20,000 BC

No bear or lion ever raked him up,
the five-year-old child,
victim of illness, accident or sacrifice,
buried in a cave floor
high above a white-walled, roaring gorge
shortly after the ice-sheets had retreated.

Someone sprinkled his grave with red ochre,
someone tied a seashell around his neck,
someone placed a few flint blades by his side,
and under his head someone laid
the dried tail of a fox, perhaps
a white fox.

In the Textile Museum

for M. Cannon (1915–2005)

These are the cloths of Egypt:
a baby's silk bonnet,
padded and lined, and trimmed
with strips of faded,
finely-stitched
red and green linen;

a tapestry tunic ornament
with its woven image
of a woman in a short tunic
carrying a baby on her back
across a river;

a fine wool curtain
whose perfect, threadbare
blue, green and orange fish
for seventeen centuries
have flashed to and fro
through its watery weave;

I will never meet the weavers
of Antinöe on the Nile
but I remember the swish and click-click-click
of my mother's treadle sewing machine
as she bent to it, intent;
the tissue rustle of a dress pattern
as she sliced through it

with her good scissors;
her appraising eye, by the sitting-room fire,
as she measured a growing piece of knitting
against the arm of one or other growing child,
while behind her, on a high shelf
her books of poetry,

bought before she married,
sat under light dust.

Love slips easily through the eye of a needle,
words clothe us;
not everything ends up in a book.

(Musée des Tissus, Lyon)

I wanted to show my mother the mountains –

the Bauges in deep snow,
pink in the evening light.
Why did I want to show her mountains
five years after she was dead?
She was as terrified of heights
as any eighteenth-century traveller...
Perhaps I wanted to show her mountains
because so often she had said,
Oh, look, look!

Bees under Snow

In a valley beside the black wood,
this year there are fifty-two beehives –
orange and blue cubes with zinc lids,
raised on long girders.

Last winter, under a foot of snow,
they were square marshmallows in a white field.
By a minuscule door lay a few dead bees
and one or two flew about distractedly
but the bees inside hovered in a great ball
shivering to keep warm, to stay alive,
moving always inwards towards the globe's centre
or outward towards its surface.

As much as their hunt for sweetness
or their incidental work, fertilising the world's
scented, myriad-coloured flowers
to bear fruit for all earthbound, airborne creatures,
this is part of their lives,
these long months of shivering, of bee-faith.

November Snow

Our boots creak down through a foot
of white shafted with blue. The hedges,
humped and swayed under huge burdens,
white mammoths' heads.

From under a smothered bush
to the trunk of a young oak,
runs a tiny track,
oval prints on both sides of a broken line –
someone's frozen tail.

and the young oak scatters
wide its bounty –
gold bullion on white linen.

Primavera

A first sighting,
five low primroses,
and later, near the compost,
a sliver of white among clumped shoots –
a snowdrop splits its green sheath,
and high birdsong in the hazels –
a jolt to realise that here too,
below snow-shawled Alps
with their tunnels and ski-stations,
this is St Bridget's Eve.

This is the evening when my father
used to knock three times on the scullery door
and wait for an invitation to enter
with a bundle of cut rushes, saying

Téigi ar bhur nglúine,
fosclaigí bhur súile
agus ligigí isteach Bríd. ★

Older, he told me his sisters used to vie
to be the one to knock three times
before entering with the first greening.
What ritual were they re-enacting?
Or we, in the warm yellow kitchen, suddenly full
of rushes and scissors and coloured wool-ends,

what ceremony were we weaving there,
folding the silky stalks into crosses
to hang above the door
of each room in the house,
or what do those little island girls celebrate
who still carry the *Brideóg*, the spring doll,
from house to welcoming house,

if not the joyful return
of the bride of Hades after three months of deep
wintering, if not a first sighting of Persephone
among the rushes in a wet western field?

And what caution was told in the hesitation,
until that third knock granted admission,
what fear of deception, of late frosts,
of February snow and dead lambs?

Our fears are different now,
of floods and fast-calving glaciers,
of birds and beasts and fish and flowers forever lost
and the earth's old bones pressed for oil.

But our bones still bid her welcome
when she knocks three times,
when she enters, ever young,
saying
Kneel down,
open your eyes
and allow spring to come in.

---

* '*Téigi ar bhur nglúine, / fosclaigí bhur súile / agus ligigí isteach Bríd.*'
('Kneel down, / open your eyes / and allow Bridget to come in.')

The Tube-Case Makers

(Les Ephemères)

This one-inch mottled twig
is built of silk and stone.
Inside it, under a larva's translucent skin,
are shadowy, almost-ready wings,
a heart that pumps and pumps.

For two or three years
it trundled about
in the shallows of a mountain river
in this stone coat, eating leaf-debris,
adding, as it grew, a little sticky silk
to one end, a few more tiny stones,
until the time came to shut itself in,
to almost seal both ends of its tube –
as intent on transformation
as any medieval anchorite.

It is not true that it
turns into a green soup
but how does it happen,
the breaking down of redundant muscles,
the building of flight muscles
as a grub becomes stomachless,
rises out of the river,
for one summer's day, to mate,
alight at nightfall,
and lay the eggs
that have kept its tribe alive
since it rose in clouds
around the carbuncled feet of dinosaurs –

with each tiny,
down-drifting egg
encapsuling

a slumbered knowledge
of silk,
stone
and flight?

Fly-Catcher

Last month, Doris, the bird-bander,
told us about a one-legged bird, a fly-catcher
who traced the spine of the Appalachians
year after year, and flew south,
balancing her tiny, tattered body
down through Mexico
all the way to South America
and back to the same Philadelphia hedgerow

to draw breath among cat-birds and orioles,
to be caught in the same birders' net,
to raise brood after brood, and then
to balance on a twig,
on her single, fettered leg,
to feed on passing insects,
to store fat for her next Odyssey.

Life can be so rough,
yet we can't get enough of it.

Keats Lives on the Amtrak

for Jim and Kathy Murphy

Today, on the clunking, hissing, silver train
between Philly and New York,
the African-American conductor squeezed himself
into the dining car seat opposite,
genially excused himself and,
when I responded, asked why my novel
was full of page-markers –
'You have it all broken up' –
and I said that I was teaching it.

He leaned forward, smiled, and said,
'I'm going to get a t-shirt with
Keats Lives on it. This time of year,' –
he gestured towards the window,
trees were blurring into bud –
'when everything starts coming green again,
I always think of him...
A thing of beauty is a joy forever,
Its loveliness increases, it will never
Pass into nothingness; but still will keep
A bower quiet for us...'
I told him that it was a Dublin taxi-driver
who first told me
that Keats claimed his only certainties were
the holiness of the heart's affections
and the truth of imagination.

He took a ballpoint from
the pocket of his uniform jacket,
wrote down the quote,
asked where it came from,
as I had done, two decades earlier
in the back of a taxi,
as hundreds had

since the young, sick apothecary
penned it to his friend.

'That is a bombshell', he said,
'I'm going to give that to my little girl tonight –
Oh, light-winged dryad…'
The intercom announced *next stop, Trenton*
and the steel wheels began their loud, long scream.
He hauled himself up out of the seat,
smiled again and, drawing a line
across his chest with his thumb, said,
'*Keats Lives*'.

At the end of the flight

from Dallas to Philadelphia
the flight attendant announced
that we had the father and sisters
of a fallen soldier on board,
that we were to remain seated
until they disembarked,
that she had died honourably.

There was a round of applause
and another on landing;
a middle-aged man in a beige jacket
stood to take down his hand luggage –
a carrier-bag with the corner
of a folded, starry flag poking out –
and two young women in jeans
rose from separate seats
further down the plane
and we heard the sound of grief
grinding three separate tunnels
through their days.

Snow Day

Snow
like manna
fell through the night.
By my closed window
the cypress's fingers
strain under mounds
of white.
Deep deer tracks
pass the front door,
halt at the hedge,
start again, deeper,
at the other side.

Snow fell and fell
through the night,
feeding our need
for silence,
for mid-winter light,
for believing that all can be
cleansed,
made right.

Do the Sums

The last of the brown-headed matches
that filled the box so snugly
rattles about on its own;

the tideline wears a fluttering feather boa –
shed, feather by curved feather,
from the breasts of a hundred swans;

the tap, dripping all night slowly
has filled the basin to brimming;

so why am I astonished
to find myself over fifty,
at least half of my life gone.

Shrines

You will find them easily,
there are so many –
near roundabouts, by canal locks,
by quaysides –
haphazard, passionate, weathered,
like something a bird might build,
a demented magpie
bringing blue silk flowers,
real red roses,
an iron sunflower,
a Christmas wreath,
wind chimes,
photographs in cellophane,
angels, angels, angels
and hearts, hearts, hearts
and we know
that this is the very place
the police fenced off with tape,
that a church was jammed
with black-clad young people,
that under the flowers and chimes
is a great boulder of shock
with no-one to shoulder it away
to let grief flow
like dense tresses of water
over a weir.

At Killeenaran

for Carol

We stood in a curve of seaweed
in light grey rain
with our jacket hoods up,
watching two seals
that hovered just beyond the tideline.

Their eyes were as calming as those
of a pair of Byzantine saints
gazing at us from an icon screen.

Then we turned about
and saw a sky-high arch,
all seven colours humming,
both ends firmly planted
in the ebbing tide of the estuary
and outside, above it,
in the blustered clouds
a bigger arch, very faint,
but absolutely there.

Lament

Let me learn from the Brent geese
their grey grammar of grief
as they wheel in a bow-backed flock
onto a February tide.

Let me learn from these strong geese
to map my losses with a cry,
learn from those who are always losing
a chick, a lover or a brother,
losing one cold country or another.

Let me learn from the black-necked geese
how to bend my shoulders low
over a wrack-draped shore,
let me learn from the curlew's long weep,
Oh, oh, oh, oh, oh.

Classic Hair Designs

Every day they are dropped off
at Classic Hair Designs,
sometimes in taxis,
sometimes by daughters,
often by middle-aged sons
in sober coats
who pull in tight by the kerb,
stride around to the door
and offer an arm.

How important this
almost last vestige
of our animal pelt is.
How we cherish it –
the Egyptians' braided bob,
those banded Grecian curls,
the elaborate patterns of Africa,
the powdered, teetering pompadour,
the sixties' long shining fall over a guitar,

and the fine halo
of my almost-blind
ninety-two-year-old neighbour,
permed and set
in the style
in which she stepped out
with her young man
after the last World War.

Genius

There is a man who polishes the brass handrails
of the curved staircase in the National Library.
He polishes them often, and with great attention.
They shine like the brass kettles that
were polished weekly, on a Tuesday
or a Thursday, then put back like soft lamps
onto the sideboards of old people's homes.
I greet him. He smiles and keeps shining,
rubbing off the drying green polish.

When I borrow books
I sometimes find that the writers
who wanted to dream a nation into being
or forge its conscience
or reveal its hypocrisies, have sat
and read at these same green tables.
They have all walked up the same staircase
holding or leaning on the brass rails
which are brazen serpents,
curved bands of light.

The man who keeps the rails gleaming,
who brushes up the rain-soaked leaves outside,
has written no books.
He is a genius of care,
the genius of the place.

Clean Technology

In the spring of '92
the French government,
in consultation with Doctor Antoine Louis,
Secretary of the Academy of Surgery in France,
entrusted the construction of the first guillotine
to Tobias Schmidt, maker
of clavichords and pianofortes.
He proposed a slanted
rather than a rounded blade,
tested the machine on animals
and on human corpses
till it sang.

In the summer of that year,
when he applied for a patent,
the ministry of the interior refused him –

It is repugnant to humanity
to issue a patent
for an invention of this nature.
We have not yet reached
such an excess of barbarity.

Molaise

Odd that he should be quartered here
where regiments mustered and marched
and orders were barked at straight-backed men.
His gaze has outlasted sword and fire,
the quiet gaze that fell for seven centuries
on the lintel and jambs of his stone house
and – when he was carried out, shoulder high –
on Sliabh League, Ben Bulben and Knocknarea,
on the deep walls and the speckled stones
of Inishmurray, where pilgrims made their stations
hoping to shed their agitation, if not their cares.

What drew me to this stillness
on many damp Dublin Saturdays,
my spirit at seventeen or twenty
a turbulence, a lurching boat?
I knew nothing of stormy Inishmurray,
its monks and poitín-makers,
but was drawn to this oak sculpture
with the cheekbones of an Asian sage.
Sages were almost as suspect as saints
but Molaise was quiet as a Henry Moore
and touched the same ground in me.

And who was the artist carved it
seven centuries after the battle at Ben Bulben
fought over a book's copyright,
seven centuries after, legend asserts,
Colmcille came to Molaise in remorse
to receive a penance of green martyrdom
which sent him to Iona in the north?

Where did the sculptor learn his art?
And who was the commissioning abbot?

– eager, perhaps, to draw a pilgrim trade
away from Armagh, Derry or Lough Derg –
a businessman maybe, who dealt
in curses and blessings, or maybe not,
for the corrupt middle ages were also the age
of Francis who listened to wolves and birds,
Hildegard who healed and left us songs,
and Julian who tells us "All shall be well".

I, now in middle age, am past denying
that I have known women and men
in whose presence I am calmed and blessed,
under whose compassionate gaze I am complete
as the storm-rounded stones on Inishmurray's beach.

www.annalsofulster.com

When my O Canannain ancestor
pillaged the sanctuary of Lough Derg
in the eleventh century
and carried off its gold vessels,
he could hardly
have foreseen that letters
put down carefully
by some tonsured scribe
would light up on a screen
a thousand years later.

How could he have
divined the power
of an inked feather,
of the quartz seam
ticking under the heather?

The Singing Horseman

The white horse, with its golden
chest and head, is from another world,
is kin to wide-winged Pegasus,
or to the white horse that carried Oisin off,
or to the black mare of Fanad
who saved her rider from a demon.

But this golden-headed rider is one of us,
a young man with a torn red sleeve
jogging home, bareback, from the races
on a breezy summer's evening in Sligo,
riding near the rough blue shore
heading north towards Streedagh,
playing a whistle or singing,
and the painter, who paints them both,
is an old man who remembers a hundred races,
a hundred summers' evenings.

But how are we, who do not believe
in magic steeds, to understand this,
except to remember the years
between fifteen and twenty-two
when our spirits strained as a moth's
wings strain inside its brown, spun prison,
when a song – pressed into black vinyl
        by some Dylan, seeking his direction home,
        or sung by an acquaintance at a party,
        giving voice to some long dead passion –
released our crumpled spirits,
transported us across skies and oceans
and our hands, our heads,
were golden.

(National Gallery, Dublin)

Treasure

Yesterday among green-shouldered reeds
I found a treasure – no young Moses,
but a water-hen who steered six fistfuls
of black down through a motley of shadows.

Disturbed, she made for her nest,
stamped loudly on its dry reeds
and pecked the slowest on its bald crown
as it grappled its way up.

In an empty nest this morning
the red-gartered cock hauls in dry stalks
to build up a small round Venice;
it sinks daily on its brittle pylons.

A bright-beaked clockwork toy,
he motors upstream to the canal bridge
where his mate guards their long-toed chicks;
they clamber over broken reeds and bottles.

A tiny black frenzy paddles behind the hen
as the parents call them all out into the bright
heat at the edge of the reed-bed.
Only one was lost in the night.

Three Mountain Gaps

The crooked gap, high
on the shoulder of Derryclare:
across it, a rapier of pink light.

The V-shaped gap at the end of Gleninagh
through which, at winter solstice,
the sun sets, now a little off-centre,
to brighten an alignment of white stones –
a bog-abandoned calendar.
Today, from a nearby peak
we look down through the gap
to the sea and one small island.

The glacier-rounded gap beside Loch Ochoige,
where, earlier, as we clambered up the slope
a heron, soft-winged pterodactyl-shadow,
passed over our heads,
through its upside-down,
triumphal arch.

Eavesdropping

Late at low tide, one June evening,
at the tip of a green promontory
that brimmed with lark song and plover cry,
on a slab of damp granite encrusted
with limpets and barnacles, I lay down,
laid my head down in that rough company
and heard whispers
of a million barnacles,
grumbling of a hundred limpets,
and behind them the shushing
of the world's one
gold-struck, mercury sea.

Kilcolman

...great force must be the instrument but famine must be the means, for till Ireland be famished it cannot be subdued...

(A Brief Note on Ireland)

In my palm lie three rabbit bones
picked clean by an owl who carried them home
to this last tower of a castle where a poet
praised his queen in limber verse,
where every bank now brims with primroses
in a spring that is late and most intense.

Here cattle fields are electric-fenced,
mallard and moor-hen nest on the lake
and steps descend to a covered well;
here, the adventurer knew little peace,
gave little in return, but laboured to praise
the power that brought him into this place.

From here his grandson would send to Lord Cromwell,
a plea against banishment to Connacht,
would claim that, having come to the age of discretion,
he had renounced his mother's popish religion,
that in that province he would be placed in peril
as his late grandfather's writings *touching
on the reduction of the Irish to Civilitie*
had brought upon him *the odium of that nation.*

How barbarous the price of courtly ways,
The castle torched, a new-born child dead,
the poet dying in London *for want of bread*;
earlier, the slaughter at Smerwick
and in subdued Munster the Irish, starved and sick,
*Creeping from their wooded cover on their hands,
for their legs would not carry them.*
How hard, even still, to love the well-turned verse,
whose felicities were turned on such a lathe.

St Stephen's — a Speculation

On an April morning two young women
plant a poplar tree in St Stephen's Green.
In a grid of straight streets
the fingernail curve of St Stephen's Street
with a tall hotel at the far end
traces the northern edge
of a lost monastic enclosure; its bell
rang out over a black pool
before Viking ships made landfall at the Long Stone.
The enclosure came to hold St Mary's Abbey
and the leper hospital of St Stephen
which owned a grazing green to the east
through which, many centuries later,
a fictional student
of the same name would stroll out
with real hands sunk in his pockets
to become almost as real as Hamlet.

He strolled out well after the Liberator's time,
after the hospital had been renamed
and St Mary's Abbey replaced with a soaring nave
under whose altar lie the bones of St Valentine,
a Roman martyr, portrayed with an orchid,
as his feast day replaced the shepherds' spring feast
of Lupercalia — and who knows what ritual site
the lost monastery might have replaced
near the meeting of four great roads,
what shepherding of fertility and death,
what grove of sacred trees
above a black pool.

The Sum of the Parts

It was partly the collage of regrowth
displayed in front of the small library,
in a city that has suffered greatly –
an image of green tendrils,
softening the oblongs of tall city blocks;
and it was partly the welcome
of scented candles floating in glasses
and the words on a screen beside them,
words carried across oceans and the reefs of language;
and it was partly the graciously-offered cup of wine,
and the grandmother who humoured
a little boy, pretending to bite his hand
as he tugged at her gold earring;
and the young, smiling pair across from them,
and the mentally disabled man
who found it hard to listen but who listened anyway –

but it was mostly the two women who arrived late,
their white canes tapping either side
of the narrow aisle of the library auditorium.
They walked up to the front with their guide
and had space made for them in the first row
and afterwards asked us to write our names in ink
beside raised Braille,
which left us humbled, honoured
to be servants of the word.

(Biblioteca Fernando Gómez Martinez, Medellín, Colombia)

The Hang-Gliders

for Jean O Donnell and Nico Bernier

This afternoon we saw them,
huge rainbow-coloured butterflies
high above us as we swam in the lake –
so many sons of Daedalus
who, in search of that ever-longed-for lightness,
run and jump off a cliff,
steer themselves about for hours in the air,
skim mountain ridges,
levitate on thermals
and, almost always,
avoid assumption into storm clouds.

Later we pass them, two-legged mortals
in shorts and t-shirts
who solemnly lay out their sails in the shade.
They fold and pack with exquisite care
each cord, each of the pleats
on which their lives depend, in order.

I recall the huge butterflies
I saw in the botanic gardens
emerging from their upside-down capsules,
first the head, then the strong legs
pressing against the papery cockpit lid,
and then, tumbling out slowly,
those exquisitely crumpled wings.

Acoustics

Those tall medieval cathedrals
were set as nets for light,
built as sound-boxes
for psalms, for praising choirs.

When I open my back window wide
it is clear that my small room
was built to tremble with the tune
of a treetop blackbird in June.

The Greening

The mountains, the built-up valley,
drink the sky.

After a full night of summer thunder
rattling from one end of the sky to the other,
of lightning and rain battering
the hard, cinnamon-coloured earth,
everything dreeps green again.

Clouds hunker among the summits
of lower mountains
and the high Alps are hidden.

Grass stands up again in the garden
as tree-furred mountainsides drink up,
bringing the sky's dark
into every leaf tip,

and already
under bare summits
gentians have turned thunder
into blue velvet.

Antrim Conversation

Chalk is stained brown near the waterfall.
It crumbles away easily
as flint nodules are prised free;
the flint itself is poised
to split into slivers,
a suggestion of blades,
a memory of the trade
this sharp wealth engendered.

The small, tidy man who paused on his stick
to talk to us in the lane,
on this Sunday of rose-hips and blackberries,
had a voice soft as chalk.
He spoke first of weather and houses and sheep,
of a life working *to put wee shoes on wee feet*
and we talked on and on in September sunshine
until nodules of hurt washed out
in the stream of his words.

He spoke of being shaken awake as a child
by uniformed men with guns;
of his own young son beaten up;
of prison, of *not knuckling under,*
and then of his satisfaction on hearing
a man's head had been blown off
in a neighbouring town.

History's hard cart rattled on
as flint nodules shattered
into narrow weapons.
We wondered, dumb,
what shift of bedrock,
what metamorphosis,

might heal such wounded,
wounding ground.

What do we know of the chalk,
the flint, of others' souls
or of our own
or of what might break in us,
if history's weight
pressed heavily down?

How do we know
that we could hold the pain
and not pass on
the false and brutal coin?

Moment

Within our sliver of the earth's time, was his
a moment in the evolution of our blue globe
akin to that moment when a tiny
multi-legged creature dared to live out of water?
A man who kept repeating, *forgive, forgive,*
be not afraid, be not afraid, a man
who had a god for a parent, as had Achilles,
but no god-given armour.

Did his death mark the end of the heroic age,
or had the age of heroes already waned
as Homer forged his song of ships
and valour and flame-wrapped Troy
and Hector hauled behind a chariot?
Did that blind man set Priam's love in balance
forever, with Achilles's strength and pride?

Hadn't Siddhartha already ridden out
and seen and felt and taken to himself
the wretchedness of all the earth?
and weren't there others before them
struck by some inner or outer light
whose compass was compassion and love?

Was this his triumph, to say it again,
in all those parables to say it again and again
and, knowing the red trough that awaited him,
to put back that struck-off ear,
to bless, not the victorious and the strong,
but the peacemakers, the meek?

Galanthus

Head down
spring's small white herald
gallant in green stripes and chevrons
braves the mud and gales
of January.

Viewing the Almond Blossom

This was an exercise the Japanese poets
repeated every year
as though some lessons could not be
well enough learnt –

how a brown twig puts out
small pugilists' fists
which open, fragrant burst
after fragrant burst
right to the stem's tip.

The Collar

In the corner of the vast, captured mosque
of Abd al-Rahman –
a spreading forest
of salvaged Roman pillars, Arab arches,
and a cathedral like a perched stork –
in the cordial city, where for a time
Muslims, Christians and Jews lived
and worked in amity,
above the locked iron gates of a chapel
dedicated to the Virgin Mary,
we saw a small, dusty medallion
containing a castellated coat of arms,
the inscription *Ave Maria, Gratia Plena,*
and a turbaned moor
chained in an iron collar.

And the mosque
began to fill
with the clatter of crusades,
aroma of the baked crescents of Vienna,
stink of the mass graves of Srebrenica,
the dust of the toppled towers of New York,
hum of drones over Pakistan,
the clank of that collar-chain
and weeping of those who were chained
and who chain in turn –

many victories,
many collars,
little grace.

(Córdoba, 2013)

Alice Licht

Three ordinary shoe brushes in a museum case,
the kind of brushes whose soft swish
I used hear every morning –
my father 'feeding the leather'
of his creased brown shoes.

The Reich needs brushes, the half-blind
Otto Weidt insisted, thumping the table
of a Berlin police station
and I need my Jews to make them.
Give me back my Jews.

With the help of his ally,
the policeman,
he got them back –
those blind and deaf Jews
and some he pretended were blind and deaf.
He led them back in a long line
like children holding hands,
children released
from a door in the mountainside,
to Rosenthaler St.,
where they worked for two more years
making brushes, binding brooms,
in his small factory in the *Höfe*
with its narrow rooms
painted with pink and green borders,
with its windowless room at the end
where he hid a Jewish family.

And once he drove in his car
to the gates of Auschwitz *to sell brushes* –
as if any brush could clean a hell-floor –
his purpose being to carry back

three Jews, a young woman – Alice Licht –
and her parents.

The parents died
as did, in the end,
all the blind and deaf brush-makers,
in spite of Otto's ruses and bribes.
They were swept up one morning
late in the war,
by men in shining boots.

His message
was passed to Alice Licht
and she, at last,
escaped to Berlin,
stood at his window
as the war ended,
a small light,
like courage
or blind hope.

Bilberry Blossom on Seefin

for J.

Halfway between mist and cloud,
we saw it by the barbed-wire fence –
pink-edged boxwood,
and the flowers, rosy cats' bells,
so round and waxy we took them for berries
but May is too early.
And after that there were low clumps everywhere,
the tiny bells secretive as nipples.
It bloomed through last year's heather
up near the summit,
where we unwrapped our sandwiches
as wind sheared through an empty tomb

and I imagined the bilberry-pickers
who used to climb the hills in August,
long-dead boys and girls –
cattle-herders, butter-makers,
singers, dancers – brash and shy
as any disco- or club-goer
and full of the tug of summer's long desire.

And on our way down, just across the path
from a storm-flayed swatch of pine
grew great clumps of the pink and green bushes.

And later still
as we drove down the mountain road
they grew tall along the verge,
so we pulled in and picked big bunches
to carry home
all the ringing promise
of that blossom and leaf
we had often seen before
but had never heard.

Notes

Molaise (page 37)

A thirteenth-century wooden statue of the sixth-century Irish saint Molaise was, until the 1950s, kept in a building known as St Molaise's House, in the monastic settlement on the island of Inishmurry off the Sligo coast. The statue was traditionally removed from the house and venerated on the saint's feast day. In the eighteenth century an attempt was made by Loftus Jones of Ballisodare to burn it as an idol. It is currently housed in the Collins Barracks section of the Irish National Museum.

Acknowledgements

I thank the editors of the following publications in which some of the poems have previously appeared:

Agenda, Archipeligo, Five Points, Temenos, Poetry Ireland Review, Cork Literary Review, Earthlines, Irish Pages, The Irish Times, Ropes, Windows, The Stony Thursday Book, Lines of Vision, An Ghuth.

I wish to warmly thank Charles A. Heimbold for a fruitful semester at Villanova University. Sincere thanks are also due to Joseph Lennon and James Murphy of the Irish Studies Department and Evan Radcliffe and the faculty and staff of the Department of English, Villanova, for their hospitality and kindness. The unfailing support of the Arts Council of Ireland is most gratefully acknowledged.